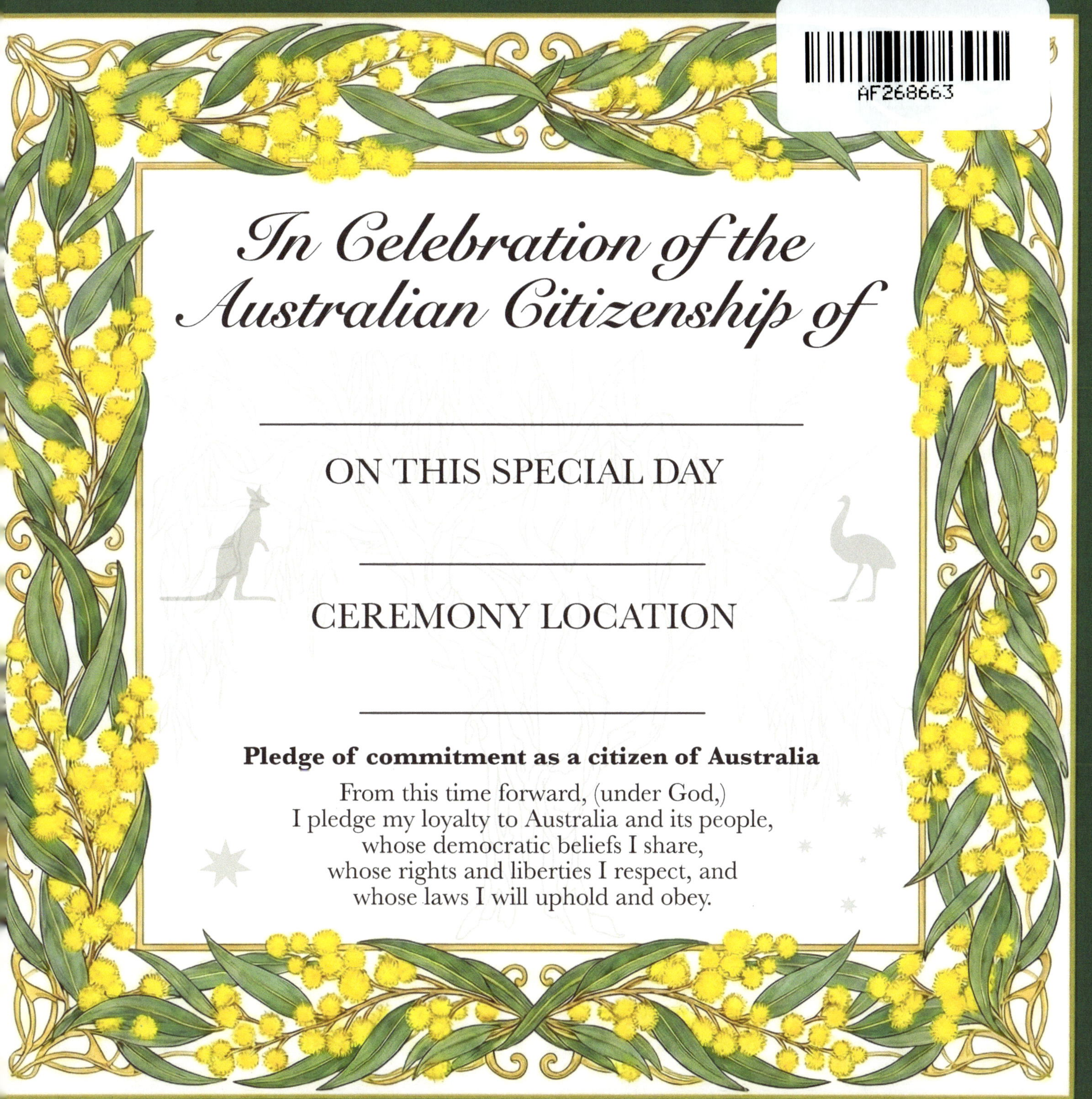

In Celebration of the Australian Citizenship of

____

ON THIS SPECIAL DAY

____

CEREMONY LOCATION

____

Pledge of commitment as a citizen of Australia

From this time forward, (under God,)
I pledge my loyalty to Australia and its people,
whose democratic beliefs I share,
whose rights and liberties I respect, and
whose laws I will uphold and obey.

A catalogue record for this
book is available from the
National Library of Australia

ISBN 978-1-7644931-0-9

Paperback edition
First edition

Daniel Griffiths

I'm Australian
My Citizenship Promise

About the author

Daniel migrated from Wales and became an Australian citizen in 2023. He later attended many citizenship ceremonies as a councillor for the City of Whitehorse.

We had waited years for this day, but it still caught us by surprise.

"I've found the invitations for the Town Hall", shouted Dad.

Everyone breathed a sigh of relief, and all the rushing slowed down.

Dad triple-checked that he had all of our passports.

I stood by the door, trying to not be the reason we were late.

Then Mum walked past, wearing beautiful clothes
from our home country, ready for our citizenship ceremony.

"Why do we have to go?" I asked. "Australia is already our home."

Mum knelt down and took my hands. "Today makes it official",
she explained.

"The promises we make today are a gift that stays in
our family forever, including your children one day."

I was still thinking about 'forever' when a magpie swooped down,
boldly landing in front of me.

It sang an old magpie song. The song felt unfinished, like an
invitation to add my own voice to the story of this place.

We got in the car and quickly drove down our street.

Past the library. Past the park.

Past my school and over the speed bumps. BUMP... BUMP!

The world went flying past my window.

It felt a bit too fast for my eyes, so I put on some headphones
to calm my tummy.

I played the song we had been practicing for weeks,
singing along in my head.

("Australians all let us rejoice, for we are one and free...")

We could see the Town Hall from the car. In the past, lots of
people had become citizens here. Today, it was our turn.

A long queue of people waited to go inside. They came from all over the world to make Australia their new home.

Everyone was excited and took lots of photos.

They wanted to remember this day forever.

I felt a little nervous, but I was ready to go in.

Inside, we found our seats and sat down together.

People kept coming in. Lots and lots of people.

All here for the same reason.

Then, the room became as quiet as a library. Everyone looked up.

It was the Mayor walking in, wearing long robes
with shining gold chains.

Other important people followed, smiling and walking slowly.

As they reached the front, I struggled to see what was happening.

I sat up as tall as I could.

I stretched my neck to see over the people
in front of me.

Right behind the Mayor stood a beautiful Australian flag.

It was full of stories.

"That's the Southern Cross", Mum whispered.
"The same stars that watch over us at night."

"But look at the biggest star of all,
the Commonwealth Star", Mum continued.

"Can you count the points? There are six for the Australian
States and one for the Territories, all shining as one."

But then, I spotted something else.

High up on the wall, was a grand picture of a King looking down at us.

"What's he doing up there?" I asked.

Mum pointed to the flag. "Do you see the Union Jack in the corner?
That's the flag of the United Kingdom".

"The King represents that part of Australia's history and still watches
over us, but the Prime Minister leads the government and country."

Before the official talking began, everyone hushed.

We sat very still.

The Mayor told us the story about the land under our feet.

"This land is very, very old. It was here before this building.
It was here before the roads", the Mayor explained.

"It was here before anything else."

"People have loved this land for a long time",
the Mayor continued.

"And today, YOU become part of this special place."

I didn't move. I listened closely.

I felt goosebumps on my arms. I knew that something important had just been said.

I was becoming something bigger than before.

Next, it was time to stand alongside my family.

We just had to make a promise.

The Mayor spoke the big, official words, and we repeated them.

In my heart, I knew exactly what I was promising:

To be a good Australian. To be kind and fair. To let people be free.
And to follow the rules.

We all proudly sang the national anthem and waved our flags.

Saying this promise
made it official.

I'm Australian, mate!

Mum squeezed my hand. "Now you can have a passport with a kangaroo and emu on the front", she smiled.

"And one day, you'll have a chance to vote in elections."

We walked up to the front. The Mayor shook my hand and gave me a small eucalyptus tree and my special certificate.

"Welcome to the big Australian family", announced the Mayor.

I held my little tree and certificate very carefully.

Standing a bit taller, I smiled the biggest smile I had.

Looking around, I saw that everyone else was smiling too.

We were all part of the same big moment.

On the drive home, everything looked familiar
but it felt different.

We dug a small hole in the garden
and planted my little eucalyptus tree.

"Now you will grow old together", Mum said softly.

That night, as the Southern Cross stars began to sparkle in the sky,
I snuggled into bed.

I thought about the big promises that we made today.

I thought about the history of the old land beneath me.

I closed my eyes... and smiled.

Now, my Australian story begins.